I0824571

For Stephanie. Every artist needs a champion,
and I'm grateful you are mine.

Margaret Quinlin Books
An imprint of Peachtree Publishing Company Inc.

Printed and bound in January 2026 at C&C Offset, Shenzhen, China.
The artwork was created with pencil, watercolor, and digital.
Edited by Margaret Quinlin and Vicky Holifield
Book design by Amy Manzo Toth
PeachtreeBooks.com
First Edition
1 3 5 7 9 10 8 6 4 2
ISBN: 978-1-68263-779-1 (hardcover)

Library of Congress Cataloging-in-Publication Data is available.

EU Authorized Representative: HackettFlynn Ltd, 36 Cloch Choirneal,
Balrothery, Co. Dublin, K32 C942, Ireland. EU@walkerpublishinggroup.com

Beatrix and Her Friends

Anne Lambelet

Margaret Quinlin Books
PEACHTREE
ATLANTA

Beatrix belonged in nature.

When everything around her was growing and changing, her heart came alive.

She listened to her
governess tell fairy stories
on their daily walks
in Kensington Gardens.

She smelled fresh-cut hay
and tasted sweet cow's milk
at her grandparents' country estate.

On her family's summer vacations to Scotland,
she saw beauty everywhere.
Every mushroom, every animal, every tree
felt like a work of art to Beatrix.
She wished her pencils and paints could capture them all.

But in London, Beatrix felt trapped.

The doors of her third-floor nursery cut her off from the plants and trees and animals she loved so much.

If I can't go outside, Beatrix thought, *I'll just have to bring the outside in.* By the time she was a young woman, Beatrix—with the help of her brother, Bertram—had practically transformed the nursery into a little zoo.

They filled it with animals from pet shops
and animals they'd caught in the wild.

There were snakes and lizards,
birds and bats.

There were frogs, mice,
guinea pigs, and rabbits.

Beatrix drew and painted them all
again and again.

One of her favorite subjects
was her pet rabbit, Peter.
She took him with her everywhere.

One year, on their summer holiday, Beatrix and her family stayed at a big house with beautiful gardens.

It was looked after by a man named Mr. McGregor.

Beatrix loved exploring the gardens with Peter.
It made her smile to imagine all the mischief he could get into.
She wondered if it might make others smile too.

She put one of Peter's adventures into a story for a little boy who needed cheering up.
Her words and pictures were a doorway to Mr. McGregor's garden.
She thought about turning her story into a book.
Then Peter would always be there.

Beatrix hoped a publisher might love Peter as much as she did. Instead, she received rejection after rejection, but that did not stop Beatrix. She decided to print some copies of her first book all on her own.

It was only a small book for small hands, but its instant success caught the eye of a young publisher named Norman Warne.

Norman and Beatrix worked together, and finally *The Tale of Peter Rabbit* was ready for publication. By the time the little book was in bookstores, Beatrix was catching Norman's eye as well.

As Beatrix and Norman grew closer, he got to know her animal friends too. Beatrix loved a beautiful dollhouse Norman had built for his niece. She told him how funny it might be if her pet mice, Tom Thumb and Hunca Munca, found themselves in such a fancy home. Norman began sending the mice little doll furniture and doll food and even built a new little house for them.

Beatrix decided to put her tiny friends into a story called *The Tale of Two Bad Mice.* Now Tom Thumb and Hunca Munca would always be there to keep her company.

With Norman's encouragement, Beatrix put more and more of her animals into stories. They inspired the characters of Benjamin Bunny and Squirrel Nutkin, Mrs. Tiggy-Winkle and Jeremy Fisher. It was nice always having her friends there for her. Soon Beatrix began hoping that Norman would always be there for her too.

When he asked her to marry him,
Beatrix couldn't have been happier.

But, one month later, Norman got very sick. Sadly, there was nothing the doctors could do to save him.

Beatrix's heart was broken.

Through her loss, she found comfort in the love and friendship of her animals.

With their help, Beatrix did her best to keep going.

Using some of the money from her book sales,
Beatrix bought herself a farm.
It was old and needed a lot of work,
but it was a good way for her to return
to the countryside, to nature,
where she'd always been happiest.

When Beatrix moved into the farmhouse,
she discovered that it was overrun with rats.
That might have stopped some people, but not Beatrix!
The rats just reminded her of her old pet, Samuel Whiskers.

She decided to put Samuel into a story.
Now he and his greedy family would
always be there to make her laugh.

Gradually, with hard work,
the farm came alive around Beatrix.
She filled it with more and more animals.
There were sheep and pigs, ducks and dogs.
There were cats and rabbits and foxes.
With her friends all around her,
Beatrix's heart came alive again too.

Every now and then, Beatrix would tuck another friend into the pages of a story. But she began to wonder if stories were enough to keep them safe.

All around her, she could see the countryside she loved disappearing, little by little.

Beatrix began buying up land near her farm.
She preserved the ponds where the real Jeremy Fishers lounged on the banks. She preserved the ancient forests where the real Squirrel Nutkins frolicked in the branches. She preserved the fields and the brush where the real Peter Rabbits and Benjamin Bunnies scampered and played.

Throughout her life, Beatrix's animal friends had always been there when she needed them most. They gave her their companionship and love. They gave her their stories.

Now she was able to give them back their homes.

Thanks to Beatrix, her friends
will always be there waiting.
And they'll be waiting for you too.

Beatrix's Timeline
1866
Beatrix Potter
is born.
1871
First family
vacation to
Scotland.
1893
Beatrix puts Peter
Rabbit in an
illustrated letter to
Noel Moore.
1901-Beatrix self-publishes
The Tale of Peter Rabbit.
1905
Norman dies and
Beatrix buys
Hill Top farm.
1913-Beatrix marries
William Heelis.
1927
Beatrix sells fifty
drawings to save the
Windermere lakefront
from developers.
1930
Beatrix publishes
her last little book,
The Tale of Little
Pig Robinson.
1943
Beatrix dies, leaving behind
twenty-three beloved children's books
and 4,000 acres of protected land.

I have always loved the stories of Beatrix Potter: the timeless characters, the lush settings, the beautiful illustrations. Her tales were whimsical in a way that sparked my imagination, yet they were also full of rich details that made Beatrix's secret animal world seem real to me. As I researched this book, that feeling of "realness" became even more evident.

Peter was based on Beatrix's real pet rabbit, Peter Piper. The characters Tom Thumb, Hunca Munca, and Samuel Whiskers were all based on her pets too. But Beatrix put many more of her "real" friends into her books. Mrs. Tiggy-Winkle was based on her pet hedgehog, who apparently started to bite if expected to pose too long for drawings. Jemima was the name of an actual duck at Beatrix's Hill Top farm, and Jemima's rescuer in *The Tale of Jemima Puddle-Duck* is none other than Kep the collie, Beatrix's favorite farm dog.

Other characters and settings might not have had real-life counterparts, but they were still almost always drawn from Beatrix's surroundings. For instance, in the summer of 1903, Beatrix painted many scenes in and around Fawe Park, where her family was vacationing. St. Herbert's Island in Derwentwater became Owl Island in *The Tale of Squirrel Nutkin* and a little squirrel she tamed became the model for Squirrel Nutkin himself. Similarly, in preparation for *The Tale of Pigling Bland*, she described trying to draw one of the pigs at Hill Top farm. Although she referred to the Hill Top pigs as her "six pink cherubs," this one seemed to have gotten on her nerves a little.

No matter the challenges she encountered drawing them, the genuine fondness Beatrix had for these animals always came through. In one of the early copies of *The Tale of Peter Rabbit*, Beatrix inscribed the following:

> *In affectionate remembrance of poor old Peter Rabbit, who died on the 26th of January 1901 at the end of his 9th year . . . whatever the limitations of his intellect or outward shortcomings of his fur, and his ears and toes, his disposition was uniformly amiable and his temper unfailingly sweet. An affectionate companion and a quiet friend.*

Pets like Peter weren't just animals for Beatrix, they were her companions. Her stories are a patchwork of the companions and places Beatrix treasured most. They reveal the love she felt for her animals and their native homes. I hope that reading my book will lead you to seek out more of her stories and will help you know and love Beatrix—and her friends—a little better as well.

Anne Lambelet

SELECTED BIBLIOGRAPHY

The Beatrix Potter Society. https://beatrixpottersociety.org.uk.

Graham, Beckett, and Susan Vollenweider, hosts. *The History Chicks.* Episode 64, "Beatrix Potter." The History Chicks, LLC, March 26, 2016. Podcast. https://thehistorychicks.com/episode-64-beatrix-potter.

Lear, Linda J. *Beatrix Potter: A Life in Nature.* St. Martin's Griffin, 2016.

Taylor, Judy. *Beatrix Potter: Artist, Storyteller, and Countrywoman.* Narrated by Patricia Routledge, audiobook, abridged edition. Penguin Audio, 2012. https://www.audible.com/pd/Beatrix-Potter-Artist-Storyteller-and-Countrywoman-Audiobook/B009SCYFHA.

Zach, Emily. *The Art of Beatrix Potter: Sketches, Paintings, and Illustrations.* Chronicle Books, 2016.

Left: Beatrix Potter aged fifteen with Spot, the family spaniel, at Hill Top, Sawrey. Photographed by her father circa 1881. © National Trust Images
Right: Beatrix Potter with her pet rabbit in 1891. WorldPhotos / Alamy